44 Secrets for Playing Great Soccer

Mirsad Hasic

DEDICATION

I dedicate this book all soccer players around the world.

CONTENTS

ACKNOWLEDGMENTS

I would like to thank my family for their support.

1 KEEP IT SIMPLE

I can promise you one thing, and that is if you learn to keep things simple, you WILL succeed! This is something that cannot be emphasized enough.

To become successful on the soccer field, and improve your chances of becoming a professional player, then you must acquire the ability to play the ball on the first touch. And while this may seem obvious, most amateur players do not do this because they don't realize how powerful it actually is.

The ball will be always faster than you. Even Olympic gold medalists can't compete with the speed of a ball!

To illustrate the true power of 'first touch', spend some time watching professional soccer games. It doesn't matter which team is playing, but it should be a professional soccer league so that you get to see talented players in action.

You then need to try to count the amount of one touch passes. I can tell you now, this is going to be pretty hard to spot.

Professional soccer players don't have time to mess around with the ball as they might do when having a game of backyard soccer with friends.

In professional games, each little mistake can cost the team greatly, so there simply isn't time to work on the best approach.

The greatest players on the earth, like Lionel Messi and Cristiano Ronaldo, as two examples, play the ball on the first touch, and if you are serious about upping your own game, then you should be doing the same?

One general rule is to never touch the ball more than twice while you are on your own side of the field.

Once you form this habit, you will be able to play a safer game, more efficiently, and without risking unnecessary mistakes. Although it may sound pretty obvious in principle, a lot of players do tend to overcomplicate this.

How many times have you seen a player who receives the ball near his own 18-yard box, and then starts performing some fancy moves, just to show the crowd how skillful he is? My guess, is quite a few!

Don't be one of those players who become focused on selfish aims and never play for the team as a whole. These guys are out to seek their own glory, and care little of jeopardizing the results of the club.

Again, if you are genuinely serious about advancing your soccer career, and have aspirations that go further than just playing friendly matches with friends, or for local community clubs, then you must learn to play the ball on the first touch!

2 TWO STEPS AHEAD

If you have ever played chess, then you will understand the importance of trying to figure out your opponent's next move. In fact, a good chess player will endeavor to determine what the next several moves are likely to be, so that they can plan their own actions better.

The reason for this forward thinking is simple. If the chess player fails to figure out the opponent's next moves, then they will more than likely lose the game! This very same principle applies to soccer too, therefore it's really important that you understand the true value of developing this skill.

If you don't learn to plan ahead, you will probably lose every time (unless your opponents are equally as casual). So try to be constantly mindful as to why the ability to think on your feet is so incredibly important when it comes to soccer.

A good player will always attempt to think two steps ahead before even receiving the ball. So the faster you can figure out what to do with the ball, before it even touches your feet, the easier it will be to perform well on the field.

If you study the professionals, you'll notice how they seem to have eyes in the back of their heads, and how they are adept at reading the game and the players very well.

If these guys hadn't mastered the ability to figure out their next move(s) long before they received the ball, then they wouldn't be playing at the level they are.

The higher tempo of the game, the more important it is to know what you should do with the ball before it arrives at your feet.

Attempting to receive, control, and turn around with the ball as two opponents are rushing towards you like mad bulls, might work with backyard soccer (where your friends are not so aggressive and hungry to tackle you as soon as they get the chance), but there's no time for this in highly competitive games where there's a lot at stake!

Try it once and you will realize how quickly you can get hurt, frustrated, and even snubbed by your team mates, especially when you start playing against really fast and talented players in important matches.

Soccer is not only a physical game but a mental competition too. And just like chess, each maneuver must be carefully evaluated before making important decisions.

Put into practice what you have learned in this chapter, and I can promise that you will notice some real improvements in your next game, and the games that follow that.

3 BE RELAXED

When I started to play soccer and participate in regular competitions, I found myself getting really nervous and anxious just before and throughout each match.

I played really well during practice sessions, but as soon as a real game started, my confidence disappeared. In fact, it got so bad that I'd start running around illogically and avoiding the ball whenever possible because I was afraid of making mistakes and letting the team down!

At the time, I was completely at a lost because I couldn't figure out what to do about it, until one day I remember just pausing and saying to myself, *"That's is it, enough now! I don't care if I lose the ball or make mistakes during the game. I'm just going to start relaxing from now on and enjoy the matches."*

As it turned out, this was the best decision I could have made. Suddenly, I was playing with renewed confidence and people started asking me: "Hey, what's happened to you, and why have you never played like this before?"

Although my greatly improved performance was due to hard practice and dedication, none of that would have materialized on the pitch if I hadn't adopted a new attitude and made a conscious effort to relax on the field.

The lesson I took from this was simply that the more nervous you are about making mistakes during your game, the more mistakes you will make.

You may think that you can hide yourself on the field during times of lost confidence, but you are still highly visible from the sidelines. If you are uneasy, your coach, fellow players, and everyone else will notice. And should you continue like this, it could see the end of your place on the team.

So here's what I suggest: Imagine your next game as a playground; a place where you can have some fun. Let go of any negative thoughts, and only think about how much enjoyment you're going to have for the next 45 minutes (it's psychologically better to break the game down into halves at the start of your new approach).

I know this is easier said than done. Our minds are can be complex at times, and that means forming new beliefs isn't quite as simple as flicking a switch.

So despite your longing to relax more and have fun, it might be a bit of a struggle for some to remove that old negative thinking pattern, but it can be done, and it won't take long to adjust, providing you desire the change.

Remember, you must really believe in having fun, and you can't just pretend to enjoy the game while your legs are shaking! This is not a 'fake it till you make it' approach, it has to be your genuine belief that you're only playing because you want to, because you love the game, and because it's FUN!

The time has come to now relax and enjoy your way to soccer success.

4 KEEP YOUR MOUTH SHUT

Did you know that your performance on the field could decrease by more than 50% purely by focusing on the wrong things? For example, arguing with the referee, or opponents, is something that you should avoid at all costs!

Even if you are so full of adrenaline that it's seems impossible to avoid getting angry when a situation arises, it's crucial to know that you will not gain anything positive by acting out, and no, it's not - as some suggest - a simple case of 'letting off steam'. Physical or verbal aggression on the pitch never adds anything positive for you or the team.

The only thing you'll earn yourself is a yellow card or, even worse, a red one, which will mean that you are out for the rest of the match.

The only thing you'll earn yourself is a yellow card or, even worse, a red one, which will mean that you are out for the rest of the match, and probably slammed by your coach and team mates too.

I used to play with an amazingly talented player who was three times better than me from a physical perspective. However, his main problem was that he just couldn't keep his mouth shut.

So this meant that instead of being a good 'team player', he ran around and argued with the opponents at every given opportunity, and that did nothing to help the side – nothing!

It wasn't unusual for him to earn himself a red card because of his constant protesting and confrontations with the ref.

The only reason our coach put up with his bad behavior was because this player was so talented, and we could just pass the ball to him and let him work his magic. In fact, there was one season where he scored a total of 56 goals, which is amazing no matter what league you are playing in.

It wasn't too long before the bigger local clubs started to scout him, and he finally got drafted for a second league club, where he starting earning a salary to play soccer.

Despite this amazing opportunity, he still couldn't control his behavior on the field, and this inability to manage his manners showed up at his very first second league game.

The coach gave him few chances to work on his conduct, but his behavior only got worse over time. Not surprisingly, after only a few months he was sacked and sent packing back to our team.

He continued on the same path, still full or talent yet lacking as a good 'team player' simply because he kept letting the side down with his mouth. After a few more years he decided to quit due to lost motivation and his inability to control himself on the field.

He never played soccer again after that, not even in friendly community type matches. It was sad to see a young man waste his talent and a real chance of playing in the higher leagues, and for what? For no other reason than his failure to control his behavior.

The reason for writing about this is to point out the importance of focusing on your game, and to avoid becoming someone who argues and debates on the pitch!

Even when you are fit to burst, for whatever reason, restraint is they key here. If you don't, it will not only have a negative impact on your performance, but you will put your team in a bad situation as well.

Worst of all, is that you might even lose an opportunity of being drafted, because after all, you never really know who is watching your games!

5 FINDING MOTIVATION

Practicing and working on your skills can be tough, especially when you don't seem to be achieving the desired results.

What's even worse is when you notice your teammates seem to be doing everything right during practices sessions and games, while you, on the other hand, are struggling to improve one whatever skill it is you're working on. It's times like these where it becomes easy to lose your motivation.

Don't worry, I'm going to show you how to maintain motivation. I will now describe how I developed the best crossing passes in my team.

When I started to play soccer, cross pass seemed to be rocket science, at least to me it did. I mean, how was I supposed to kick the ball more than 30 yards without having it touch the ground?

I practiced this skill day in and day out, but I simply could not get the desired results. In fact, my crossing passes were a joke, and I became really discouraged by this.

Each time we had a training session that included passing, mine were really terrible, while my teammates seemed to perform this particular skill without any real effort. Yet, despite it all, I did not give up!

I wanted to quit many times though, and my friends often wondered why I was always practicing by myself while they were either enjoying swimming or playing video games.

It took me a whole year to master this skill, and that was a year where I practiced daily, come rain or shine, but I got there, in the end!

As we returned from our summer vacation that year, I noticed something that absolutely delighted me: My cross passes had become perfect. My teammates were envious and couldn't understand how I went from being so bad last season to so good this one.

Dig deep to find the motivation needed to reach your goals, and then stick to your plan, come rain come shine come hell or high water!

And whatever you do, never listen to anyone who tells you that you will never be good enough!

6 ACCEPTING BAD WEATHER

It's easy to avoid practicing when the weather is not perfect and find excuses to do something else like playing video games, or watching TV.

I will be the first one to raise my hand and admit that I've done this on quite a number of occasions during my soccer career.

Of course, practicing in icy cold, or wet and windy weather, is nowhere near as gratifying as playing soccer on a nice warm, bright, summer's day, but, you can't control the weather, nor should you let it control you.

Instead, you need to simply accept the fact that the upcoming training session may be really tough if the weather is particularly bad, but staying indoors, as tempting as it might be, will do nothing to improve your game.

Have you ever practiced in minus 10 degrees Celsius while the snow is falling and you can barely see your teammates? I have. In fact, I've practiced in this kind of weather for as long as I can remember. If anything, it toughened me up and made me a better player.

In Sweden, where I come from, the winter runs from November until the end of April, giving us a predicable six months of winter weather, and there's no such thing as a mild Swedish winter!

I can't even describe how it feels to train when freezing rain is falling in the middle of December, along with biting winds. Yet despite it all, we just turn up to practice and get on with it.

There are three simple strategies that I use to prevent me obsessing about bad weather, which consequently stop me looking for copouts.

1. The first one is to warm up properly, and I really do mean you should break a sweat as you would if you were running on a warm, sunny day!

2. The second strategy is to simply forget about it and focus completely on the practice. Believe me, the more you try this, the easier it will become.

3. And finally, I keep myself moving all the time. This means I never stand and watch during drills. Instead, I am constantly moving around to keep my body warm and the cold out.

It's impossible to change the weather, so if you can't beat it, then why not join it?

Try not to complain and keep going on about it, because if you do, you're only setting yourself up for finding justifiable excuses that will be used to avoid attending soccer practice in the future.

Instead, take it for what it is, and get out there and start doing your best. You will glad you did.

7 READING THE GAME

Reading the game is not the same as reading a book (just to clear that up in case you don't already know). Reading the game means figuring out what your opponent is likely to do.

For example, imagine that a winger is about to cross the ball to the other winger. In this case, you would properly position yourself to where the ball will likely be passed, and either gain possession of it or clear it away.

Another example of reading the game is to figure out what your opponent is about to do next.

I'm sure you have been in situations when you know that your opponent is about to pass the ball to a nearby teammate, and then you moved in to block that pass and regain possession of the ball.

These two situations are clear examples of how to gain advantage on the soccer field by reading the game.

If you allowed that winger to keep control of the ball (because you hadn't read his anticipated moves), then you wouldn't be able to get possession of it.

Instead, the winger will either try to challenge you in a dribbling duel, or play the ball to a nearby teammate, and you would therefore have a much harder time of stopping him!

The ability to read the game is not something you can practice on your own. It must be done during games.

The reason is simple, in that you need match situations to improve your ability to read the game. This is what coaches often refer to as *"the game without the ball."*

You will probably only have the ball at your feet for a total of two minutes per game, if that! This is the average time you will have to pass, shoot, and receive, etc.

For the other 88 minutes you will need to cover for your teammates, mark your opponents, and..., you've got it, 'read the game'.

In order to achieve higher standards and become a better player, you will definitely need to develop an aptitude for reading the game.

8 BEATING LAZINESS

Have you ever felt that you would rather sit in front of the computer or watch a movie instead of going to soccer practice?

Join the club! I've been there and done that too, and in all honestly, if it hadn't been for my father insisting that I go to practice, then I would have missed many more training sessions because of my laziness.

A lot of people say that procrastination is the hardest habit to crack, particularly in today's technological society where there are so many idle distractions.

But you will only get out of anything what you are prepared to put into it. But almost always, people feel much better after making an effort to do something than when they don't.

This is the same for soccer; you can't expect to become a successful player if you don't put the hard work in. It's just not possible to practice only when you feel like it, and expect to excel in your game.

You have to go to practice if you're serious about becoming the best you can be, even when it is the last thing you feel like doing.

Laziness is a state of mind that you need to get rid of, so why not change your mindset, starting today?

You have to promise yourself that you will never miss another practice because you are too tired, too busy, or just too lazy. The only time you can justify missing training is in the event of an illness, injury, or an emergency of some description.

At the end of the day, you are playing soccer because you want to reach a higher level than just backyard games with your friends, right? So if you are deadly serious about upping your game, then your mind has to be in the right place – always!

I know that it's really easy to come up with an excuse for skipping practices, and if you want to find a copout as to why today is not a good day to train, then you will come up with a plethora of excuses. We humans seemed to have mastered the art!

I used to come up with all kind of excuses that seemed perfectly justifiable to me at the time. These would include such things like having too many chores to do at home, or too much school work (a classic one that!).

While in reality, I would more than likely hang out with friends and play computer games, or watch a DVD.

Another classic was to complain about having stomach pains, knowing that I'd really be sitting in a fast food restaurant eating pizza just minutes after making the excuse.

I want you to read this until you really get it. You are not fooling anyone with your excuses for avoiding soccer practice, only yourself!

9 KEEP YOUR EYES UP

Keeping your eyes up separates the professionals from the amateurs.

If you study a skillful player like Messi or Ronaldo, you'll notice how they rarely keep their focus on the ball. In actual fact, they barely look at the ball during a match.

Both of these players are humans, just like you and me, with the only difference being is that they are super skilled at soccer.

So just how do they achieve such amazing levels of ability on the pitch? Have they got some secret formula for mastering it, or is it simply raw talent?

Well, obviously they have a talent, but this alone is not enough. No, their secret (if you can call it a secret) is that they have spent thousands of hours on improving and shaping their skills and techniques, and the only reason they've been able to do this is because they're passionate about soccer.

The final product is what you see on TV or live at the stadium. Their ability to control the ball without looking at it, is not something they picked up by sitting around and playing computer games.

I will be the first to admit that this skill is one of the hardest to learn, and it requires countless hours of practice.

If you pay attention to your teammates, you will see that most of them run with their eyes completely focused on the ball.

This means they don't have a clue of where you, or your other teammates are on the field. It is only when they slowdown that they are they able to look up and try to figure out what their next move should be.

If you keep your focus on the ball, then you will often find yourself running into opponents, which is not something you want to be doing!

One of my previous coaches used to force us to run in different directions on the field, while keeping our gaze upwards, and without looking at where the ball was.

This was not an easy task at all, and we often managed to run only 2-3 yards before losing control of the ball completely .

I also stumbled on the ball dozens of times, as did the others, which made us look pretty funny at the time. But this 'stumbling' also revealed to us just how difficult this useful skill was to master!

However, I first understood the real power of this when I started to become more proficient at running with the ball and not having to constantly focus on it.

As a consequence of this, I was suddenly able to read the game easier too, and that meant finding teammates on the field who were best positioned to score from my passes, but I also improved my own scoring ability as well!

If your plan is to play higher up in the league system, then you will need to master this skill.

10 DON'T JUST STARE

As a continuation from the previous chapter, if you really want to know where your opponents are, then you can't just stare at the ball.

Imagine that you are playing in the position as a fullback, and the ball is played from the wing by one of your opponents. Now, you don't want to just stare at the ball here, because if you do, then you would not have a clue of where it is.

An opponent can easily sneak up behind you, and as the ball approaches your feet, he could simply get an opportunity to kick it and score.

I say again, if you study professional soccer players, you will notice how they rarely look at the ball.

This is highly visible during a corner kick where players are responsible for keeping a watchful eye on their respective opponents.

If a player makes the mistake of staring at the ball, instead of keeping the focus on his opponent, it will make it that much easier for the opposing team to take control and potentially score.

Obviously you need know where the ball is, but it's less important than knowing where your opponent is and anticipating his moves!

I've lost count of how many times my team lost in the past, for no other reason than we were all watching the ball during those corner kicks and free kicks.

Even if we marked our players, there was always someone who thought: *"Umm, the others will probably mark him, so it's better if I just concentrate on the ball."*

Playing against skillful teams, will mean it's impossible to win if your side only focus on where the ball is.

If you truly want to play at a higher level and get to realize your soccer ambition and dreams, then start to studying professional players to help reinforce this method into your mindset.

11 SCORING & CONFIDENCE

Do you ever dream about becoming the top goal scorer on your team and having opponents fear you because of your skills? If so, then you need to work on your confidence.

Scoring goals is all about having poise and confidence; and without these essential attributes, you will have a hard time putting that ball into the net with any real frequency.

It doesn't matter if you have the most powerful and accurate shot on your team, if you don't believe in yourself when there's an opportunity to score in a real game, then you will fail to realize your true potential on the field.

Have you ever watched a game and heard the commentators saying something like: *"He really needs to boost his confidence. If only he could just could score a goal, I believe he would gain it back."*

Even the pros can lack in confidence, or lose what they once had due to a few knockbacks. Read about Fernando Torres, as his career is a good example.

He used to be a real goal-scoring machine for Liverpool, but once he joined Chelsea, he barely managed to hit the goal post, let alone get the ball into the net.

From being the true star of his team, he suddenly found himself sitting on the bench.

Though this may seem a bit extreme, you need to remember that professional soccer is all about results, and when a player stops delivering the goods, there is no other option but to give him a back seat until he ups his game, if indeed he can bring himself back.

If you fail to deliver what is expected of you enough times, then you will get sacked. And if you don't score, you will not get to play very often, especially if you are a striker.

Once confidence is lost, it can be hard to get it back. It's a phase that all soccer players go through at some point. Some manage to pull themselves back from the brink, whereas for others, it's the end of their career.

The sooner you recognize a loss in confidence, the sooner, and easier it will be, to work on getting it back, or better still, becoming even more confident than you were.

Whether you are playing as fullback, midfielder, or striker, you must believe that you can score, even if you know that you will rarely get a scoring opportunity because of your position.

A player who can score is worth more than one who can't, it really is as simple as that. So make sure to take advantage of every chance you get to score a goal. Seriously, scoring goals can literally take you from the bottom directly to the top of your game!

12 YOUR WEAK FOOT

Have you ever tried to handle the ball with your weak foot and felt that it was like trying to play soccer with a golf club?

I felt this way when I started to practice on my weak foot. I remember thinking, *"Is this really my leg?"*

In the beginning it was really tough, comical sometimes too, although the funny side soon wore off as the frustration kicked in.

Heck, I had to try really hard just to strike the ball without having my foot dig into the ground at every attempt.

During practice sessions, I strove to use my weak leg as much as possible, even though it irritated my teammates because most of my passes often missed them by several yards.

However, things started to improve and I learned to pass the ball with all parts of my weak foot.

I also started to use this foot during our shooting exercises, but I could not score because the power was just not there, although it was much improved on what it used to be!

I initially lacked the confidence to demonstrate my skills during actual games.

Then, one day when we met one of the strongest teams in our league, I found myself about 30 yards from the opponent's goal as the ball came bouncing towards me at perfect speed.

Without any hesitation, I made a perfect kick with my weak foot, and got to see the ball land beautifully in the left corner of the goal.

I was shocked that I had actually scored with my weak foot, but overjoyed nonetheless! And what a goal it was too, even though I do say so myself.

And this is why you should work on your weak foot as much as possible. After all, two feet are better than one, especially when the weaker foot plays a stronger role than one of mere balance.

Follow my advice, and you will definitely be able to play better overall, score more goals, and take better advantage of opportunities on the field as they arise.

Make no doubt about it, when you first start working on your weak foot, you will feel as if you've borrowed it from someone else, and the ball will bounce off in all directions, without you having too much control over it.

However, stick with it and don't get discouraged. After a while, your coordination will improve and the foot will start to feel like it belongs to you again.

I can tell you now, I would never have scored that goal if it wasn't for the improved dexterity of my weaker foot, nor would my ability on the field be what it is today if I had neglected to work on it.

I would even go as far to say that the goal scored with the weaker foot was perhaps the most beautiful one I have ever netted!

13 TRUE TEAM PLAYER

A true team player will always strive to encourage his teammates, even when they are struggling or failing to do well.

There is nothing more demotivating than having a fellow player complaining about your performance all the time.

Furthermore, this fault-finding will often spread like a virus through the whole team, then before you know it, you will have several of your teammates arguing with each other about all kinds of trivial nonsense.

By encouraging your teammates, especially when they are struggling, or appear to be letting the side down, you will increase their confidence and help them to move on and get over their setbacks.

When I first started to play soccer, all the other guys on the team were far more skillful at the game than I was.

Just receiving a pass without having it bounce away several feet in the wrong direction, felt like an impossible task as I was learning to master my game.

I remember this one guy, who constantly complained about everything I did on the field.

I didn't care all that much about this in the beginning because I thought 'ribbing the rookie player' was just par for the course. However, I have to admit that after a while, his constant griping really started to bother me big time.

He began to gnaw on my nerves so much, that I started hearing his cantankerous voice even when I wasn't directly involved in a game. It's almost as if I'd allowed him to come and live inside my head, rent free!

Every time I touched the ball, I did something stupid, and even when I didn't have the ball I was doing something wrong, like forgetting to cover my players, or not moving up fast enough to release our offside trap, among other things.

I can remember vividly the day when this guy decided to quit the team, and how a few days later someone else joined to take his place.

The replacement was a really good player, and I recall how I admired his skills with the ball. Best of all though, was that he was a nice guy, someone with patience, tolerance, and a real team player (quite opposite to the one who quit).

During his very first game with us, this new guy started to encourage me, especially when I made mistakes (and there were several of those!).

Even when I caused a penalty, he said, with a wink: *"Don't worry; we will score in the next attack."*

His attitude really motivated me, it really did, and believe it or not, I somehow managed to score a goal, which felt pretty amazing.

I know now that this was down to feeling energized as opposed to demoralized, and at last I felt like a part of the team instead of feeling apart-from it.

My point is this: you will never win anything by complaining about your teammates.

Instead, make them better by encouraging them, and especially during those times they make mistakes.

I don't care who you are, it is my firm belief that a pat on the back, and a few words of encouragement goes a long way. This is what soccer is all about: team spirit!

14 BEING SELF-CRITICAL

Self-criticism is one of the most disturbing and irritating things I ever experienced during my soccer career. Sometimes we are our own worst enemies when it comes to nit-picking our faults.

But thinking we are the bees knees is equally as damaging, and that is what this chapter is about.

Having someone running around screaming at you in a negative way every time you have the ball, is a real pain!

Perhaps you are someone who constantly criticizes your teammates, while at the same time think you are the perfectionist on the team, the one who never makes any mistakes?

For a lot of people, it's much easier to find fault in others than it is in ourselves, but self-criticism, or perhaps self-assessment is a better term, is necessary if you want to improve your own game.

So try to be honest now. Can you really look at yourself in the mirror and say:

"Well, I actually play my best, but my teammates are really bad, so it's not my fault that we lost this game and all the others, it's down to them because they can't get their act together"

I bet you can't say that if you are being totally honest, and I will tell you why:

If your team is losing a lot of games, there's a very good chance that you too are playing poorly, but are taking out your frustration on your teammates, instead of looking at your own game with total sincerity.

There were times, once I thought I'd earned the right, where I'd complain about my teammates for every little mistake made on the field.

The consequence of this was that we'd perform worse than ever because of my constant critiques. In fact, I had become somewhat similar in nature to the very guy that used to demoralize me when I first joined the team. Go figure!

My advice?

Stop doing this now!

Promise your teammates that you will encourage them even if they create five penalties in the row, or better still, don't say anything, just do it!

Being self-critical is not about diminishing your confidence, it's about taking honest appraisal of any shortcomings you might need to work on.

Try to identify any weaknesses within yourself, analyze them carefully (without beating yourself up), and attempt to figure out how to improve them during the next practice.

Don't be afraid to ask for a little guidance too, if you think it will help.

Grab a notebook and list five mistakes – if you can – that you made in the previous game.

Write down what you plan to do in order to improve on, or avoid repeating these slip-ups next time, and then save those notes for reference.

Now, before you set out for the next game, read this list over a few times so as to become mindful of the points prior to kick-off.

And during the game, try to remember what you read earlier, and then follow through on your plan of action as best you can.

For example, if you won five heading duels and lost 10, try to increase this number to seven, keeping a focus on why you might have won the ones you did.

This is a tactic I have been using during my entire career, and it really works well.

You may find that it's hard to be honest with yourself in the beginning, as you try to own up to your mistakes on the soccer field, but the more you do it, the easier, and more productive it becomes, I promise.

15 SHOOT TO SCORE

When I started to play soccer, I was really afraid of shooting, but I dreamed plenty about scoring goals, as I'm sure you did or still do.

Obviously dreaming doesn't work without following through on your thoughts. I mean, if you don't shoot, you will never score. It's as simple as that!

I started to work on my shooting skills as much as possible during practices, but practice wasn't my setback. It was the actual games where I was still afraid to put into practice what I had learned during the training sessions.

One day, my coach asked me: *"Mirsad, why is it that you never shoot when given the opportunity? I mean, you really have a powerful shot, so why not take advantage of it?"*

He said that I really had a powerful shot, and thanks to those few words of encouragement, I started to shoot during games with renewed confidence. Not long after that, I scored a memorable first goal; a moment I shall never forget.

From that point on, I scored more and more important goals for my team, and I can't begin to tell you what a rewarding experience that was.

This was a dream come true, it really was. I went from being someone who never scored, to having my teammates believe that I was the one who would decide the outcome of our games.

This is great for the ego, but far more important than that is my valued contribution to the team as a whole, which is what soccer is all about.

My desire to help the team by scoring more goals for us, helped me improve my overall game too.

I simply could not have done this without taking positive action, and by using my shooting skills to their full potential.

This was something that had been there for quite some time, yet needed that little bit of encouragement from my then coach in order to materialize.

So I suggest you to do the same, and that is not to think, just do! Just tell yourself if he can do it, then I can too.

By changing your mindset and thinking like a champion, you will soon realize that you can score more goals than you ever thought possible! Think BIG and great things will come to pass. Think small, and you will remain a smalltime player.

Remember, if you don't shoot, you can't score!

16 EYES OPEN & HEADING

I will be the first one to admit that keeping your eyes open during heading duels is not easy at all, in fact, it can seem quite impossible at times!

For some reason, our mind automatically encourages our eyes to shut as soon as the ball makes impact with the head.

Even professional players tend to close their eyes during a heading duel, but the most successful ones are able to keep their eyes open, therefore giving them a great advantage over those who don't.

This is one skill that you can easily practice with a friend. Simply throw the ball up in the air and then both jump for it as you try to win the duel. Remember to focus on keeping your eyes open as you compete for the header.

Hopefully, after some practice, you will be able to convince your brain to keep your eyes open during regular games. Mastering this will prove to be a huge advantage, both for passing and goal scoring.

Another benefit of keeping the eyes open when going for a header is that there will be less chance of collision, thus reducing the risk of potential head injuries.

I never realized how good I could be until I stopped closing my eyes during heading duels, and my teammates marveled at the way I would win almost all of my heading duels, even against really tall players.

I told them that there was no big secret here, and all they needed to do in order to improve their own heading duels is to just learn to keep their eyes open no matter what!

17 BENCHED, NOW WHAT

One of the most frustrating moments you can face as soccer player is getting benched during a game.

I know how it feels because it's happened to me on a number of occasions in the past.

All any player wants to do is jump into the game and give it their all as they strive to do their bit in helping the team win. There is nothing worse than being at a match realizing you are not going to be a part of it - this time!

OK, so you have to accept the bench situation and just prepare yourself for the next game, but then you discover that you are still on the bench, and the coach refuses to let you play, despite your pleading.

I can tell you that the minutes spent on the bench can feel like an eternity. There are dozens of thoughts flying through your mind, as you hope against hope you will be called by the coach at any moment.

You think that by getting into the game you will really get to show everyone just how good you are, and how keeping you on the bench was a big mistake.

But too long on the bench, too often, then other, more negative thoughts will visit your mind.

You may start to doubt your talent, and zoom in on how poor your skills must be compared to those of your teammates. You get to thinking that the coach is perhaps doing the right thing by keeping you on that bench after all.

So, what can you do about this situation? The answer is simple, and that is to focus really hard at doing your very best during practice sessions. Furthermore, take every chance you get to improve your current skills (including any free time you have outside of training), and show your coach that you really do deserve another chance.

If you continue to sit on the bench, then it's time ask your coach if he plans to let you play in any upcoming games.

If the answer is no, then I would kindly ask for permission to switch teams because being on the bench is not only demoralizing, but it does nothing to help you improve as a player.

A new team, and team environment, can boost your confidence, and as we've already discussed in an earlier chapter, having confidence improves your game, and in this case, it will increase your chances of playing too.

I agree that this is a drastic change, particularly if you get on well with your fellow players and are passionate about the team as a whole. But if your aim is to play higher than amateur soccer, then you will need to make sacrifices.

So, are you prepared to take the necessary steps to reach your objectives, or do you want to be stuck on the bench forever? You have read almost half of this book now, so I think we both know what your answer is.

18 COUNTER A SLIDE TACKLE

Imagine approaching the opponent's goal, and just as you are about to release your well-aimed missile, an opponent slips in from the middle of nowhere and slide tackles you.

Of course, he manages to clear the ball away and you realize that your chance of scoring this time has suddenly vanished.

Or has it?

Well yes, but only if you let it happen!

The solution here is a preventative tactic called 'countering a slide tackle'.

What this simply means is that you avoid the tackle from happening by figuring out your opponent's next move (see the chapter on 'Reading The Game').

This is also a great way to protect yourself from potential injury, since slide tackles are in general hard to control, which means that opponents will often slam into your legs as well.

There are three strategies I use to counter a slide tackle. The first one is to basically jump over the opponent.

The second is to decrease my speed, or stop running altogether, and allow the opponent to slide past me. And the third tactic is to keep my eyes up. In other words, I focus on the players, not the ball.

Remember, we have already looked at why focusing solely on the ball is a bad idea. When you don't know where your teammates and opponents are, you are much more likely to lose control of the ball, and that could secure you a place on the bench!

Keeping your eyes up is probably the most important talent to become proficient at here. If you are able to master this one, the other two will automatically be added to your arsenal of skills.

Unfortunately, the slide tackle accounts for many serious injuries on the pitch, and sometimes it's really hard to avoid, especially if you are attacked from behind; something that often results in a red card for the opponent.

You have to remember that soccer is a collision sport, and that injuries are an unfortunately a part of the game.

This is why you need to be completely prepared and focused during each and every match.

So besides trying to play well, you also need to do everything you can in order to avoid getting injured.

19 MORE KEEP UPS

Many rookie players want to know how to increase their keep ups. Well, it's no different to any other soccer skill, in that it's practice that leads to improvements, so the more you train the better you will become at it.

While this might sound like a bit of a cliché, if you really focus on improving your juggling every day, I can promise you will soon notice some amazing results.

Progress might seem slow to begin with, but stick with it and your skill is going to jump to a whole new level.

I really wanted to improve on that number, but felt it was just too hard, or that I just lacked the talent for this particular skill, so I eventually gave up trying.

Then one day, as my friend and I were playing backyard soccer, he asked me: *"Mirsad, how many keep ups can you do?"* My response was. *"Well..."* (I was unsure what to say).

He then told me that his record was 89, and asked me once again, how many could I do?

I told him that I'd never actually bothered counting, and suggested we should cut the chitchat and get on with practicing our passing skills!

Inside I felt completely discouraged, because my friend

was almost at 100 keep ups while I couldn't even get past 10. What made me feel even worse is that he started to play soccer at the same time as I did.

A few days later, this feeling of discontent left me, and actually turned out to be a positive thing. My competitive streak unveiled itself and I started to relentlessly practice my juggling technique day in and day out.

I spent at least 30 minutes every day working on my keep ups and in the beginning it was really hard, just as it was when I first tried. However, the difference this time was that I refused to quit, and after a few weeks I managed to perform 20, then I increased it to 50.

Not long after that, I was able to break my friend's record (something that was an impossible thought just a few months previous), but it gets better.

One year later I was able to perform 500 keep ups, which was really amazing considering that just 12 months prior to that I could barely do 10!

When I got to about 15 years of age, I was able to perform 3,500 keep ups, my personal best.

The most important lesson I took from this is to really focus on the task in hand, and to put in the time and effort improving one juggling skill at time. The outcome will surely amaze you!

Once I learned how to juggle the ball with my feet, I then went on to learn how to do keep ups with my head. I then continued practicing with my thigh, heel and so on.

You won't get anything for free in soccer, and there are no shortcuts. Just like anything else in this life, if you really want to succeed at something, you have to work hard at it.

20 PASSING YOUR TRYOUTS

So, the tryouts are approaching and you are getting more and more nervous about them. How do you think they will go? Are you confident you will you finally make the team?

When I'm asked for tips on passing a tryout, I always start by encouraging people, telling them to go all out and give it everything they have because there's nothing to lose.

Just remember, that you never get a second chance to make that first impression.

Now, you might be thinking: *"What are you talking about Mirsad? I have everything to lose if I don't make it!"*

But what most soccer players don't seem to realize is that we do need to experience some amount of failure in order to succeed.

In fact, every professional player and soccer superstar has had to overcome numerous hurdles to become what they are today. I say again, there can be no success without some failure!

Take Lionel Messi as an example. He is seen by many as one of the best, if not 'the' best player in the world, yet he was actually diagnosed with growth hormone deficiency.

This simply meant that his body didn't grow properly for his age.

When aged 13, he was the height of an average eight year old boy, but he didn't allow that to stop him, and as they say, 'the rest is history'. Now the whole world knows who Lionel Messi is!

Not everything will not go smoothly during your soccer career either. It's got nothing to do with you personally, it's the same for every player, and these peaks and dips are all par for the course.

With that in mind, you must have confidence in yourself and really believe in your skills. This is what separates the winners from the losers, and if you want to win, then start believing in yourself!

Finally, start preparing yourself for any upcoming tryouts. It's never too early to get into great shape and improve on your skills, so don't waste any opportunity to train, or be fooled into thinking you have time on your side.

These tips may sound cliché, but the fact is that most hopefuls never put them into practice, and this is why so many talented players never gets to materialize.

Take the time ahead of time, and I guarantee you that your chances of passing tryouts will improve greatly!

21 UNFAIR OPPONENTS

Have you ever played a game where one of the opponents seemed to have something personal against you?

He would use any kind of demoralizing tactic he could, like giving you a slap when the referee isn't looking, standing on your toes during a corner kick, or just provoking you in some way at ever given opportunity.

So, what can you actually do about these types of bullyboy opponents, and is there any strategy you can use to get them off your back?

Well, you can let them get under your skin, but that means they win of course.

Or you can do what I do, which is to simply pretend like they're not even on the field, i.e., block them out of your mind and focus totally on the game.

I know it sounds like a difficult thing to do, and it can be, but this is the best strategy you can use to beat them!

When players like this realize you don't care about what they are doing (or at least give that impression), then they will simply lose interest and stop bothering you.

The worst thing you can do is to respond to their provocative behavior.

By doing so, they will know that it's working and most likely intensify their efforts to upset you, and disrupt your game!

If you are an ideal victim (as some of us tend to be for various reasons), then it will be really hard to get rid of your tormentors without them getting a red card. Therefore, I suggest you work on my proposed tactic.

In higher leagues, where they have several referees, this type of behavior is easier to prevent, since there are many more eyeballs monitoring the games.

If they see something unfair, they will report it to the head referee, who can then easily warn, or send off, a disruptive player.

22 FEAR OF BEING HIT

The fear of being hit by the ball is common among players new to soccer, and for obvious reason.

But if you are a little afraid of this, then it's one concern you need to shake off as soon as possible. And by the way, as odd as it may sound, the more afraid you are of being hit by the ball, the more you will get hit by it!

This is why I recommend you stop hiding from fast approaching balls, and take your chances of being hit, with your main focus being on what you will do with that ball once it reaches you.

Yes, I know it's easy for me to say, and when you are standing in the free kick wall, these words don't sound all that encouraging.

However, you have to man up and confront the possibility of getting struck by the ball. After all, this is soccer, and you want to play, and that means you will get hit soon or later – as we all do!

I was once hit in the face during a practice session, and I was completely unprepared for it since I was trying to cover the shot. I did hear ringing bells in my head for a few seconds as I tried to figure out what actually happened.

It hurt too, quite a lot actually, but I was able to continue the practice within minutes of the strike, and didn't have any side effects after practice.

In fact, getting seriously injured by a flying soccer ball is (in my opinion) practically impossible, but it can cause you a fair bit of pain and swelling, especially when it's a direct blow to the head!

While there have been frequent discussions and various studies on the impact of ball collisions to the head, the truth is that no one has been able to prove that people risk serious injuries by heading a ball, or being hit by one.

This isn't boxing after all, where frequent blows to the head can go on for 45 minutes.

Most soccer players, in the majority of games, are not getting smacked in the face by speeding footballs, it's just that it can and does happen from time to time.

So, if you have been running around and doing everything you can to avoid being hit by the ball, now is the time to stop.

If the ball is supposed to strike you, it will find its way sooner or later, even if you are on the bench!

23 TIMING & HEADING

While it's well known that tall players have an advantage over shorter players in heading duels, the real key to winning heading duels is timing your jumps.

You simply need to judge the path of the ball, and then jump at the precise time if you are to improve your chances of winning the duel.

A lot of players make the mistake of jumping when their opponents do, and in cases like these, the taller player usually gets the ball. You don't want to be one of these synchronized jumpers, you want to be better than them!

Learn how to anticipate the right moment before jumping, and I can guarantee your success rate will improve significantly.

A great way to improve your timing is to play the ball 5-10 yards in the air and then try to head it with as much power as you can muster.

So the aim here is not merely to make contact with the ball, but trying to use your forehead to strike it with force, in order to make it more 'real'.

While this drill is not what you might call 'fun', you do need to keep at it if you are serious about becoming a better player. Learning some skills is enjoyable whereas others can be quite boring and challenging. But great players practice them all. In fact it's the only way to improve your game overall.

The formula for becoming a skillful player is not a secret, it's all about being a dedicated all-rounder; someone who takes his game seriously and with passion.

That means the more skills you master, the better your performance will be on the pitch, which is what you should be aiming for.

24 THE POWER OF TOE KICK

A toe kick is one of the most efficient weapons for scoring goals. Yet despite this fact, you will see very few players actually use it.

This is especially true among amateur players who believe it is a rookie skill that looks bad, so they really try to avoid it whenever possible.

However, this belief is complete nonsense since it is a skill that has been used by the greatest players ever, legends like Pele, Maradona, and Ronaldo (to mention a few), so there is no excuse for you to avoid it either.

This toe kick is ideal for situations where you have a lot of opponents near you (often inside the penalty box), and where you need to finish the attack with a quick shot.

The great thing about this skill is that you can disguise it so well that goal keepers will rarely be aware of the shot until it's too late.

When I first started to use the toe kick during games, I remember being inspired by the top striker in the 1994 World Cup, the Brazilian wizard Romario.

I was amazed at how he appeared to play a simple game, yet scored goal after goal after goal.

I can remember thinking: *"If this guy is shooting with his toe all the time, then perhaps I should try this approach as well."*

In my next game, and during a corner kick, I found myself with the ball near my feet as several opponents were running towards me. I used the toe kick and scored a goal. Even if you only score one more goal, it's so worth it as you will know as a keen soccer player.

You will be pleased to know that this isn't a skill that requires a lot of practice. The thing here is just to remember using the toe kick when the opportunity warrants it.

Soccer is a game where you need to score in order to win. How you score doesn't matter, what matters is that you do!

25 MAXIMUM FOCUS

Are you one of those players who trains for the sake of it?

Do you see the training session as something you need to participate in just so that you get to play in real games? If so, then you need to change this mindset now!

Seriously, training should be just like a tournament final where you give 110% of yourself so as to help your team.

So many players don't get this. Instead they go to practice and grab every chance they can to cheat during the drills, and as soon as the coach turns his back, they start to discuss anything and everything other than the current training.

I bet there is at least one player on your team who behaves in this way, and I can tell you without any question of doubt that he will never reach very high goals!

He is just joining the practice because he has to be there if he's to get a game, when in reality he would much sooner be somewhere else, doing something completely different.

Every practice, no matter how boring or fun it might be, should be taken very seriously if you are serious about playing great soccer.

There are times where I hate working on my fitness levels by running around a field doing the various exercises. This is not my idea of fun at all. After all, I'm a soccer player not a marathon runner!

But like it or loath it, I know about the advantage I will gain over my opponents by taking the training sessions seriously, in all their forms.

And as for running, I will be in a much better position to sprint on the field when I need to. So long as I'm mindful of these facts, and understand why training is so important, then my practice sessions are all the more enjoyable.

It might bore the socks off you to watch your coach draw tactical maneuvers on a white board, but if you are to get all the benefits from all the training, then changing your outlook is the only way to go.

Soccer is the world's biggest sport, and that means there are millions of players out there competing with YOU, and only the truly dedicated will shine through and make an impression.

With so much competition around, the only way you will make it big is by either having an extraordinary talent, or by taking the harder path, and that means working on your skills with maximum focus during every practice!

Think patience, persistence, and commitment, because nothing less will do.

26 RESPECT YOUR COACH

This should be obvious, yet I have seen many players treat their coaches with little or no respect. And, to be perfectly honest, this is one of the worst things you can do as budding soccer player.

The most common reason for this is that a coach is often pumped up with adrenaline, and has to handle disappointments when a player performs below par. This means he might shout and scream in the moment, and a lot of players resent that.

But no matter what your coach says or asks you to do, arguing with him while a game is on, not only looks really bad, but it's totally ill-mannered too, not to mention noted by onlookers, which will not do your career any favors either.

I won't lie to you, I did this long ago, regrettably, but the lesson I learned is that the coach is a human being just like me, and that means he has feelings, bad days, problems, and all the rest of it.

I also came to realise that when it comes to coaching, coach knows best, and sometimes a ticking off is more than justified.

So, jumping into heated debates with your coach, especially when both of you are pumped up with adrenaline, is not a good thing to do, not at all.

Practicing restraint of tongue is an attribute well worth learning, and one that will serve you well in your career.

The best coach I had was really good at handling these kinds of situations. He simply kept his mouth closed no matter how much a player tried to argue with him.

He just knew it would look bad if he started to quarrel back, and he also intuitively knew that it was no way to settle a disagreement of any kind.

However, prior to starting a new training session, and when everyone had calmed down, he would ask a belligerent player whether he thought it was right to argue during the match, and how he thought it would look if he had taken the bait and sparked a slanging match in front of everyone.

Usually, the player would just look to the ground and respond with something like: *"Well, I don't know... I guess..."* ...and after few seconds would apologize and promise that his poor behavior wouldn't be repeated in future games.

But not all coaches are the same, and neither are all players, and sometimes things can really get out of hand.

Some coaches can seriously lose their patience and prepare to fight with those players who are letting the side down. So do yourself, your coach, and your team a favor; play your game and avoid the debating society, especially during a match! You'll be glad you did!

Heated debates, slanging matches, call them what you will, can even result in lost games because when moral gets battered, as it can do in these situations, team spirit dwindles as a consequence.

27 REVEALING WEAK SIDES

All players have their weak sides, so the trick here is to figure out what they are and use these against them.

The sooner you are able to figure out your opponent's weak spots, the easier it will be to mark him and win duels.

One strategy I regularly use to uncover the weak sides of my opponents, is to study which foot he prefers to play the ball with.

A player will always have a foot he favors, although this can sometimes be hard to determine if he happens to be two-footed.

I've often been asked whether I am left or right footed, because I can shoot with great power and accuracy with both feet. This is simply because I worked on my weaker foot when I first got into soccer.

However, it has been my experience that the leg used to perform a dribbling move, like a step over for example, that can reveal which leg is the stronger one.

Your opponent is likely to be most comfortable with playing dribbling moves using his stronger leg because this is the one he used to perform the move with from the outset.

When you identify the player's weaker foot, you can easily figure out the direction of his next move whenever he gets the ball. This means you will be able to clear the ball easier and also regain possession and reinstate a counter attack.

I use this strategy all the time, and in most cases it works great (unless, of course, you are facing Messi or Ronaldo!).

28 YOUR OWN GLORY

Have you ever played with so-called teammates who never pass the ball, shoot as soon as they get the chance (even if you are better placed), and try to claim all the glory at every match?

Well, unfortunately this is not unusual at all, and I have played with several players who were even worse than the example above.

They simply played as if soccer was a solo game, and cared little about the rest of the team. Such individuals are only there for their own selfish triumph.

But whatever they think of themselves, and their ability, I can assure you that this type of player will never reach the big arenas, and here's why:

Egomaniacs such as these will always see that ego bounce back at them like a boomerang, and quash any chances they thought they had of playing in any serious competition.

Don't get me wrong, there's absolutely nothing unethical with being motivated to perform great during your games, but you have to always be mindful of the fact that soccer is a team sport, and has no place at all for solo players.

If you can relate to the behaviors of a solo player, then you are probably more concerned with your own glory than that of the team as a whole.

So if you want to become something more than just the average Joe playing in your local league, you will need to put your team in first place, ahead of your own individual success.

If you work as a team player, your own success will come by itself. In short, the more you work for the team, and strive for its success, the more you'll get back as a player.

Just watch Messi or Ronaldo, these players are not only the best in the world, but also the undisputed stars of their team.

Yet, you will often see both of them chasing strikers and helping their team in defense (even when they don't need to do that).

29 LET THE BALL WORK

Let the ball do the work and you will succeed. I know this probably sounds really daft, but a lot of players can't understand, or don't want to understand, what it means to let the ball do the work. This is because they want to feel in control of the ball, and not the other way round.

Have you ever watched F.C Barcelona play? In most cases, they rarely touch the ball more than twice before passing it on.

You might wonder why a player like Messi should pass the ball when he can just receive it, dribble by a few opponents, and then finish the job off.

Although the above sounds doable, it's just not how things work in soccer. The ball will always be faster, even if you are Usain Bolt. No player can ever outrun a speeding ball.

Instead of running 20 yards with the ball at your feet, you should try to pass it to a teammate placed higher up on the field, as you then go and seek a new position. Not convinced yet?

Watch how Messi does it when he initiates a counter attack.

He passes the ball and then runs into a new position straight away. Now, if he was trying to run with the ball all the way, he would probably lose it, despite how good he is.

Instead he plays it smart, and forces the opponents to break their defensive line. This leaves gaps, which he can then run through and ultimately score.

You will also save yourself a lot of energy this way, since it takes more power to run with the ball than it does to seek a new position without it.

So, take my advice; let the ball do the work and watch how your game improves!

30 PICK THE BEST OPTION

Being able to choose the option best suited for you on the soccer field is one of the crucial factors for becoming a professional player.

Choosing your options means knowing whether you should dribble, pass, or shoot, once you get the ball. It is something that requires real game situations, and lots of regular practice in order to master it well.

How many times have you mistakenly passed the ball to one teammate when you had another standing in a better position for scoring? Or, how many times have you tried to dribble, when in reality you should have passed the ball?

So the idea is to know how to pick the best option for a given situation, and this requires that you carefully analyze every part of your game, and then work to improve on it.

The problem with this skill is that you can't actually practice it if you are not playing in real games. However, you can take a shortcut by playing games with friends in the backyard or at the local park.

But it is crucial that you play seriously though, as if it were a real game, as this way you get to learn how to pick the best option for the given situation.

By doing this, you will get to train your mind, thus enabling it to switch to 'best option mode'. Again, it will become much easier for you to shape this skill once you start playing regular games.

I know it's tempting to start dribbling with your friends while you are playing in the backyard, and without caring all that much if you'll lose the ball, but you will need to change your mindset if you are going to improve this skill.

With an altered outlook, playing soccer with my friends gave me the opportunity to really develop this skill. Fortunately for me, my friends were also very serious about their game and wanted to take every opportunity to improve this skill too. This meant we rarely got sidetracked.

As a result, our games were sometimes even more serious than regular matches because no one wanted to lose, and each mistake could mean defeat. So we all worked hard at avoiding any blunders during the game.

If you are aiming to really improve as a player, then it is crucial you try pick the ideal option whenever you can. You won't get it right every time, but remember, the more you practice the better you will become at deciding what the best option is when you have control of the ball.

Understanding and developing this skill will have you stand out from other players. Become really good at it, and this could take your soccer career to a higher level than you ever thought possible.

31 DISGUISE YOUR MOVE

Being able to hide your next move in soccer is a real asset because you will be able to make your opponents believe you will do one thing, when in fact you will do something completely different.

This skill is similar to acting, in that the better you are at it the more you'll get from it.

I don't mean you should become the next 007, I just mean that you need to convince your opponent, and have him believe in your deception.

One of the greatest players I've ever seen when it comes to disguising his moves, is Ronaldinho. Have you ever watched him pass?

He might look to the left, then pass to the right. Or he might look straight ahead, but actually play the ball either to the left or to the right.

He's so good at it, and never sticks to a predictable pattern, which means no one actually knows what he is about to do next.

What's really funny to watch is when opponents start running in the direction of Ronaldinho's glance as the ball takes off in a completely different path.

The only reason this works so well, is because he's able to make his opponents believe he will pass the ball one way while he actually passes it in another. He truly has become a master at this skill.

This is just a simple example of how to disguise your moves on the field, and I recommend you try this out during practices and games.

If you get good at disguising your own moves, then you will become a feared player on the pitch by opposing teams.

32 COMMUNICATION

Communicating with your teammates is a fundamental part of your game.

The sooner you realize just how powerful this is, the sooner you will discover how efficient and important it is for match performance.

To give you a clear example of how communication helps you on the field, imagine that you are about to receive a pass while you have your back turned.

In other words, you are not aware of what's going on behind you, which means you don't know whether an opponent is approaching or not.

So, when a teammate shouts to alert you, suddenly you feel more connected with the game, and can better prepare for the next move as a result of this verbal communication.

This is a simple example of how communication on the field can be extremely effectual, and improve both your performance and that of the team as a whole.

In fact, it is one of the keys points to becoming a great team, so make sure you get into the habit of doing your bit and communicate as often and as effectively as possible.

Once you get into the swing of effective communication, you will learn that there are certain words which are used by soccer players that help make a team's communication fast and efficient.

33 USING A SMALL BALL

When someone new to soccer asks me what he can do to improve his overall ball handling skills, I advise him to start juggling with a small ball.

By 'small' I don't mean you should use a tennis ball, a handball is perfectly fine for this.

Maradona could actually perform every skill with a table tennis ball, so think about that while you are practicing with something a bit bigger.

Using a small ball to improve your overall ball handling skills is no big secret. In fact, players from South America, especially the Brazilians, do this all the time.

Since many of the Brazilian superstars come from poor families, they play with whatever kind of ball they can get their hands on, and in most cases, that means something smaller than a football.

This is why their ball handling technique is as good as it is. So when they switch to a regular sized ball, the game naturally becomes much easier for them.

A small ball is not ideal for using in regular practice though, since shooting and heading the ball can be really tough, not to mention frustrating.

However, for backyard soccer, the small option is ideal. When you have plenty of time to practice, you don't need to worry about making mistakes, so just persist with this and you will improve your ball handling skills – guaranteed!

I can promise you that once you learn any skill with the small ball, you will be able to perform that same skill using a regular sized ball. In fact you will most likely perform even better with the bigger ball.

Do a search for Maradona juggling a small ball on YouTube, and you will see that this guy can actually juggle any form of orb, no matter what its size.

If you are eager to accelerate your ball control techniques, then I suggest you get a small ball and start practicing without delay.

If you decide not to use this method, I can say in all honesty that you are really missing a great opportunity to improve your ball handling skills!

34 USING A WALL

A wall can be your best friend for practicing, particularly when you are alone. Maradona used to practice relentlessly using a wall, and look how he turned out!

He simply kicked the ball against the wall and pretended it was a pass to a real player.

I admit that it's not as effective, or as much fun, as having a real person to practice with, but you need to make the best out of every situation, and it's better to use a wall than nothing at all.

Having said that, sometimes we just need to be alone in our thoughts when practicing, and the wall can be a great way for working on those passing and receiving skills, without the distraction of chatter and repartee.

It's always best to start by practicing on the weaker foot. Then simply kick the ball against the wall with different levels of power and receive it with your weak foot.

As you do this, you should practice receiving the ball with the inside, outside, and instep, of your foot.

This really is a great way to train your brain and get it used to using your weak foot.

At times, it will feel as though that foot is barely attached to your leg, but you do need to get through this discomfort if it's to become an asset for you on the field.

Another thing you can practice on is heading the ball. To do this, you can draw a ring on the wall and imagine that it is the goal.

Then what you do is throw the ball up in the air and try to strike the center of that ring.

35 KNOW YOUR DUTIES

Have you ever listened to your coach during a tactical analysis session only to realize that you have been totally lost during the games?

Don't worry, you're not the first, and you certainly won't be the last. I have made the same mistake many times over in the past.

So I've since learned that you should always ask your coach to clarify your duties on the field.

I know from experience that learning tactical jargon can be a real challenge, especially when the theoretical side is something you find hard to grasp.

And when the coach starts to use a whiteboard to explain positions, it probably gets even more challenging to follow the more he draws.

However, understand that the coach is there to help you, not confuse you.

Even if you still don't understand what he wants you to do after he's explained it 10 times or more, he will explain it an 11th or 12th time if he has to, until you fully understand what he expects from you.

Remember, the coach is on your side, and it's in his best interest too that everyone knows their role.

If he fails to do this, then he is a bad coach, period! It is his responsibility to prepare each and every player on the team for the upcoming games.

As a player, it is your responsibility for asking when you don't understand something, and shying away from this can result in letting the side down. Just realize that there are no dumb questions, only dumb answers.

If you are afraid of being mocked by your teammates for asking about something you think everyone else understands but you, then simply approach the coach later; when you get the chance to have a moment alone.

I know from personal experience that saying *"yes, yes, yes"*, each time the coach asks whether you understand something or not, is a really bad idea!

So please, make sure you fully understand what he is expecting from you in order to perform your very best on the field, for both the team and for personal gratification.

36 DO NOT UNDERESTIMATE

One of the biggest mistakes you can make is to underestimate your opponents. It doesn't matter if you know, or think you know, that they are less skilled, you should still treat them with respect, and always know that you can be surprised at any time.

When I was 18 years old, I played in the biggest soccer tournament in our region.

There were more than 200 participating teams for different age groups, and my team was the favorite to win for our particular group.

During the final game, I played as left fullback because our usual fullback was injured. And even though I was not overly familiar with that position, I still thought that my team was twice as good as our opponents.

So anyway, the game started and everything progressed pretty much as expected. We went into half time with a 1-0 lead and we were already celebrating, despite the coach's reminder that the game wasn't over yet!

When the second half started, one of the wingers was approaching me. I can remember thinking to myself, *"This guy is a piece of cake"* ...but I totally underestimated him.

He performed a really good step over, got past me easily, and then served the ball inside the penalty area. One of their strikers was first on the ball, and suddenly the score was 1-1.

Even though I was a bit taken aback (and quite impressed), I just thought it was lucky break, and that we would still win.

Yet despite our best efforts to score, their keeper made one great save after another. Suddenly, it seemed impossible to get past him.

With just a few minutes left in the game, everyone started to focus on a penalty shoot-out.

Then suddenly, the same winger got back control of the ball, dribbled past me (again), and the same striker as before scored for their team!

I was completely devastated, and failed to understand what was going on! Though I still hoped, we were in with a chance, but then referee blew his whistle and called the game.

It took me a month to get over this lost game, but the valuable lesson I learned was to never underestimate your opponents, no matter what!

37 PLAY WITH BOTH FEET

As pointed out in earlier chapters, if you avoid using your weak foot, then you are going miss a lot of great opportunities.

For some reason, those players who are left-footed seem to really have a hard time using their right foot, while right-footed players have a much easier time learning to play with their left.

Just know that by playing with both feet, you will be twice as hard to stop on the field.

The reason for this is simple, in that your opponents will struggle to figure out your next move because of your ability to play with either foot.

To illustrate the significance of using your supporting foot, just take a look at Messi and Ronaldo as prime examples.

You will see that these two players regularly use both feet to perform various skills, like shooting, passing, and receiving, etc.

The only reason they are using both feet is purely because of the benefits of doing so, and that means you should be looking to improve playing with either foot too!

If you still avoid using your weaker foot because you believe your chances are limited when it comes to passing the ball with accuracy, receiving it without having it bounce off several yards, and a lesser chance of scoring, then it's time to think again.

Practice makes perfect, and the more you use your weaker foot, the easier and more natural it will begin to feel.

The consequence of this is that you WILL become a much better soccer player as a direct result of your efforts.

Think of your weak foot as a hidden gem that you possess, but didn't know you had, and something that is just waiting to come out and play, if only you let it!

I can guarantee that your performance will skyrocket once you start using your weaker foot, and especially when you start using it without thinking.

I've said it before, and I will keep on saying it; the more you use it, the better you will play.

38 AVOID FANCY SKILLS

One of the most common mistakes amateur players tend to make is to believe that the more fancy skills they perform on the field, the greater their chances are of reaching the higher leagues.

I will be the first to admit that fancy skills are really nice to watch, but I also know from experience that they will rarely give you any advantage on the field.

A coach will always pick the player who is able to receive the ball, play it safely, and work hard for the team as a whole.

Coaches are not impressed by those who perform more like a one-man circus than a team player.

So, what exactly is a fancy skill?

Put quite bluntly, it's any type of skill that doesn't have real value on the field.

For example, it took me a lot of time to learn the ATW (Around the World) trick, but I could have better spent that time practicing my shooting skills.

Any move that can be labeled as 'no value on the soccer field' is categorized as a fancy skill, nothing more, and nothing less!

It's always nice to impress your teammates with a double ATW, or any other fancy moves come to that, but it's worth asking yourself what you actually gain from all the time and effort needed to perfect such skills?

Now I'm not saying you should never practice fancy skills. In actual fact, I like to learn a few of them myself, and sometimes it gives a nice respite from the normal stuff.

However, they should not be a priority, and your regular skills like shooting, passing, heading, and so on, must always come first if you're to improve you game on the field.

I've known quite a lot of players over the years who were impressive with their fancy tricks, but once they stepped onto a regular pitch and the real game commenced, the majority of these guys were below average.

So, if you want to achieve your soccer ambitions, start working on what's important, and not on what looks great!

39 INTERPRETING & READING

This is something that can't be taught simply because it involves real game situations.

We all know that soccer is a physically demanding sport, and that physical fitness is a must-have attribute in order for a player to be of any use on the field.

But soccer also has several connections to chess, and other games that require intellect, and here's why:

Every move you make on the soccer field will impact the result of a given decision, and the judgments made throughout the match will determining the outcome of the end game.

So there's an awful lot more to soccer than just running with the ball.

Therefore, it's important to interpret and read the game as it's played, and to try to work out your opponent's next move before he makes it.

This is not rocket science, but it will take a while before you become adept at it.

Once you train your mind into thinking strategically during games, you will subconsciously be able to analyze your opponent's moves with continued accuracy.

I can remember a few years back, when we were facing one of the top teams in the league. The game was really tough, with hard duels, and a lot of running.

I was playing as defensive midfielder, and noticed that one of the fullbacks on the opposing team was just about average at handling the ball.

He could receive the ball reasonably well, and play it safely too, but it did take him some time. I also noticed how he got stressed-out on each occasion when one of our players approached him.

A few minutes into the second half, I found myself about five yards away from him, and noticed that the keeper was about to pass him the ball. I pretended that I didn't see this.

Then just as the keeper was about to make the pass, I performed a quick run over there, and stole it from under his nose. I then had a free road to the goal, and managed to score.

This is a simple example of how I was able to interpret and read the game, by predicting what my opponents were about to do next.

You need to practice this skill in the same way, by being constantly vigilant of the opposition and anticipating their moves.

Practice this by trying to analyze every move your opponents make, and see if you can get it right, or better still, take advantage of it.

Although you will most likely need a little practice before you move in for the kill (figuratively speaking of course!).

Get good at this, and you will have a huge advantage on the field, and your opponents may get anxious just to have you near them.

Causing anxiety might sound a little harsh, but it can force your opponents to make mistakes without you even lifting a finger.

This is after all a competitive sport, and we need to use whatever skills we have in our arsenal to get one over on the opposing side, and if they fear you for your skills, then all the better it is for you and your team!

40 RESTING IS THE KEY

Many players out there are looking to improve their soccer skills, but only a few of them reflect on the importance of getting proper rest, especially the very young.

It's important to realise that the human body is not a machine, and it will not function properly if you don't give it enough rest. It really is as simple as that.

You are also more prone to injury when you push your body to work for too long, too often. So by allowing the body to rest at intervals, gives it time to repair itself, and that means you become more energized and less prone to injury as a result. This is good for you and your game.

While it's important to practice as much as possible, it's equally important to rest properly. Never forget this simple fact, or it could cost you dearly!

When should you rest?

This varies, but a general guide is to take one day off after a game. For example, if you are playing on Monday, you should try to rest on Tuesday, and then continue practicing again on Wednesday.

Alternatively, you could participate in light training (most professionals do this after every game).

This typically involves jogging, low tempo drills, e.g., soccer or tennis, and stretching exercises.

You should also analyze your environment and ensure that you can sleep well without being disturbed. Quality kip is essential for everyone, but especially for athletic types.

A soccer player should try to get about eight hours of sleep per night, although this will vary between individuals because we are all different. But eight hours is a good average to aim for.

However, it's important to note that going to bed at 10 p.m. and 2 a.m. is not really the same thing.

Even if you don't consume alcohol, you still won't be properly rested if you go to bed at 2 a.m., not even with eight hours of sleep. Don't try to cheat yourself on the importance of this simple fact.

Another recommendation for getting a good night's sleep is to avoid consuming big meals just prior to bedtime. Try instead to consume your last big meal of the day about three hours prior to hitting the sack, as this will ensure you get a good night's rest.

Just to recap then, resting to recover the body (and the mind) is absolutely essential, as it enables better overall performance and therefore helps you to achieve all of your soccer and life goals.

41 GAME WITHOUT BALL

Professional players are not playing at the top because they were just lucky enough to be in the right place at the right time. Okay, there may be a few occasions where Lady Luck played a part, but luck alone won't make anyone a great player.

Most players are successful simply because they are able to pick the best option with and without the ball. OK, granted, you can't play soccer without a ball, but stick with me on this.

The 'game without the ball' is the time you spend on the field without actually having the ball at your feet, but there's so much more to the game than just hogging the ball.

If you only have the ball at your feet two minutes per game, you still have many other vital roles to play for the remaining 88 minutes, such as marking opponents, covering up on defense, offering passing alternatives, and so on and so forth.

So the game without the ball is just as important as the game with the ball.

Several years ago I was playing in a tournament, and during the semi-final my team was awarded a free kick just outside the penalty box. I signaled to my teammate that I would take the kick.

Because the opponents were really tall, I couldn't expect to shoot the ball over them and hope for a good result. However, I did notice there was a small gap in the wall.

So, I decided to aim at that opening, and surprisingly the ball found its way through and into the goal net. Great! We were in the final now, or so I thought!

However, with about 10 minutes left in the game, the competing team was awarded a corner kick.

The opponents were running around inside our penalty box, making it really difficult to cover them, and as for me, well, I was in my own little world.

I was so happy about the goal I scored earlier, that I forgot to mark my opponent. I was already imagining how I would be the hero in the final as well (watch out for ego, it's not your ally!).

So what do you think happened during the corner kick? Well, this player performed a perfect header and scored a beautiful goal. Then, with a final score at 1-1, we lost on penalties!

The lesson learned from this is that the game without the ball is just as important as the game with the ball, and it's a lesson I have never forgot. If only I had marked that player, he would not have scored, and my team would have been in the final.

42 PROFESSIONAL PLAYERS

One of my favorite ways to discover new skills, and to figure out how to improve my current ones, is to diligently study professional soccer players.

If you really put some effort into scrutinizing these guys, you will be amazed at how many new skills you can come across just by studying their moves.

In most cases, you are emotionally involved in a game, and you don't actually care about how often a player handles the ball on the first touch, dribbles, shoots, and so on. Instead, your main concern is whether your team will win or lose.

To improve my own game, I try to avoid this mental behavior when other teams are playing. So what I do is bring along a notebook and study the guy who is playing my position.

For example, I used to play defensive midfielder, and one of the best midfielders out there (at the time of writing the first edition of this book) was Gennaro Gattuso of A.C Milan.

I really learned a lot from studying his game. I figured out that you should never be in line with the other central midfielder, and the reason is simple. If you are standing in line with the other midfielder, and the ball is played past you, your opponents will have an ideal scoring opportunity.

Obviously this way of studying professional players can be applied to any position.

I also recommend recording games, as this will make it easier to go back and review different situations as and when you feel the need.

This approach to analyze professional players can really give you some great pointers, and new ideas on how to improve your existing skills.

In order to become successful at soccer, you will need to sacrifice a lot of things, and put all your mental focus on improving your game – constantly!

There are dozens of ways for achieving this, and studying the pros is just one of them.

But you have to start somewhere, and if you don't watch carefully, and learn how to analyze those thing which make successful players victorious, then you can't expect to reach the heights of soccer stardom!

Remember also, that you can never stop learning new things, it doesn't matter who you are, or how great you think you might be; there is always room for improvements.

Even the professionals analyze previous matches of future opponents. They do this as a way of improving their own game, and team tactics on the day of the match?

43 WANTING TO SUCCEED

If you are reading this, then I'm pretty sure you are passionate about soccer. In fact, everything you do is probably related to the sport in some way.

However, the problem starts when you really want this at all costs, but there is such a thing as an unhealthy obsession.

While total dedication can be an advantage, it can also limit your performance, due mainly to the fear of failure.

In soccer, if you don't, or just can't perform persistently well, then you simply don't have a chance of making it into the big time.

It's all about playing your very best from game to game, and hoping that someone influential will watch those games and discover just how good you are.

With this mindset in place, you will sooner or later feel that your game is a battle for life or death, and this is where problems may arise.

Because you want this so badly, you focus on the wrong things, namely avoiding mistakes.

But remember what I wrote in an earlier chapter, which is in order to succeed you must fail.

To succeed on the field, you've got to have fun and allow yourself to go belly-up from time to time, and then learn from those failures.

When you really get to enjoy that time on the field, your game will relax and open up, and anyone watching on the sidelines will pick up on this.

Even if you don't score, fail to pass the ball with total accuracy, or don't win any heading duels, just continue to smile and keep on working.

If you have this mindset, you will be able to succeed at a faster than you thought possible. If you need more convincing, just find some videos on Ronaldinho playing for F.C Barcelona, and you will see exactly what I'm talking about!

This guy smiles so much on the field that you'd think that he was playing with his buddies in the backyard, and certainly not some major Champions League game in front of a full Cam Nou stadium!

44 SURPRISING MOMENTS

In soccer, the surprising moment is when you are able to perform a skill to the amazement of everyone. This is truly what separates the masters from the average Joe soccer player.

If you study the top five greatest players ever, you will notice how extraordinary they are at using the surprising moment. One of the great moments that caught my attention is when Ronaldinho played for FC Barcelona. It was during a game against Werder Bremen, and he was setting up the ball to take a free kick.

While all the players (including his own) were preparing for a shot over the wall, Ronaldinho did just the opposite. He simply took a chance and shot the ball under the wall, and it went all the way into the goal.

How magnificent and surprising was that? The opponents couldn't understand what had just happened, and even his own teammates were completely amazed at his brilliance! This is a clear example of what we call a 'surprising moment', and although it may seem pretty simple in theory, it still requires a master player behind the act for it to be executed with any real success.

ENDING...

My final piece of advice to you is as follows:

If you have a dream, do not give up on it even if someone you look up to says you can't do it.

Remember to always, always, always believe in yourself. If you don't, then those who you need to, won't believe in you either!

Be mindful of the fact that there is only one real failure in this life of ours, and that is the failure to try.

Best of luck in all your endeavors.

Mirsad Hasic

Made in the USA
Lexington, KY
20 December 2013